KV-576-790

Painting God's Beauty In Words

Poems by

Wilhma Rae Quin

To Margaret.

Wilhma Rae Quin.

Artist
Jenny Whyte

Drawings, Pgs. 50, 144
By Pamela Whyte

CJB (Complete Jewish Bible) Copyright © 1998 by David Stern, Jewish New Testament Publications, Inc

NLT (New Living Translation) Award Edition copyright © 1999 Tyndale House Publishers Inc.

AV (Authorised King James Version) The Scofield Reference Bible Copyright, 1909, 1917 Copyright renewed, 1937, 1945 by Oxford University Press, Inc.

NKJV (New King James Version) The Scofield Reference Bible Copyright © 1967 by Oxford University Press, Inc.
The Message Eugene H Peterson Copyright ©1993, 1994 1995

Hebrew spellings taken from Complete Jewish Bible, David Stern, Jewish New Testament Publications, Inc.

Copyright © 2005 Wilhma Rae Quin

All rights reserved. No part of this publication may be reproduced, stored in a retrieval system, or transmitted in any form or by any means, electronic, mechanical, photocopying, recording, or otherwise, without the prior written permission of the publisher.

ISBN: 0-9774242-4-3

Published by:
Holy Fire Publishing
531 Constitution Blvd. Martinsburg, WV 25401
www.ChristianPublish.com

Cover Design: Jay Cookingham

Printed in the United States of America and the United Kingdom

Foreword

Poetry, besides being an art form I have always enjoyed, has also become my way of crystallising the themes to be found running through the Scriptures.

God's own beauty is in His nature or Spirit, and that nature is exemplified in His Son, who is "...the visible image of the invisible God." (**Colossians 1:15**). Much of the divine nature is visible in His creation, and in the human race. The poems in this book were written to reflect all of that beauty: His redemptive plan for us; His strength given in our weakness; His healing and ministry to us while we dwell in a fallen, though still beautiful world, and above all, God's unerring faithfulness through all the darkest experiences of life.

Jenny Whyte is an accomplished artist and I am glad to have her as a friend. Wife of a Church of Scotland retired minister, mother of three daughters and a grandmother, she lives a busy life. Nevertheless, she gave up many hours to provide drawings to enhance the Scriptural quotes and the poems here. Pamela Whyte is Jenny's middle daughter.

I pray that God will bless you through this book. He has blessed me in writing it.
WRQ

"'For my thoughts are not your thoughts,
and your ways are not my ways,' says Adonai.
'As high as the sky is above earth
are my ways higher than your ways
and my thoughts than your thoughts.'"
Isaiah 55:8-9 *(CJB)*

"For the eyes of Adonai move here and there throughout the whole earth,
to show himself strong on behalf of those who are wholehearted towards
him."
2 Chronicles 16:9

"Aren't sparrows sold for next to nothing…? Yet not one of them will fall to
the ground without your Father's consent."
Matthew 10:29

The Vault

When I look up to the heavens at times
I cannot comprehend how great and vast.
They tell of galaxies, black holes and such,
of space where time is meaningless at last.

I wonder what we look like from up there,
all life on this terrestrial sphere?
He whose thoughts and ways are far above ours,
does God know and care that we are all here?

For people, birds and animals, all kinds
not only does He care for quick and dead,
His Word assures me that He knows my name,
has counted every hair upon my head.

The stars and moon that travel the great vault,
sometimes obscured by clouds, yet all still there,
tho' I see Him not as with those great lights,
He watches with a Father's love and care.

This world is poor when knowledge of true God
is spurned for that which sense makes us aware.
His Spirit like wind comes from where it will
and nought escapes His notice or His care.

For everything there is a season, a right time for every intention under heaven… a time to plant and a time to uproot…"
Ecclesiastes 3:1-2 (CJB)

Perspective

For the first time in my long-ish life
I was seeing it at first hand.
Of course, I'd seen all the bits before,
sowing, growing, harvest from the land.
But now my little pooch and I
took our daily walks together,
beside the fields throughout the year
thro' the seasons, whatever the weather.
We watched the brown fields begin to show green
'til the green eclipsed the brown
and the shades of green grew deeper
as the crops became full grown.
The warmth of the sun eventually
caused the green to turn yellow then gold,
when the harvesters came to cut down the growth
the harvest to be stored and sold.
The fields looked forlorn as, the cycle complete,
all the earth was bereft of the grain,
but after a time the sowers appeared
and the rhythm began again.

Yuri Gagarin, the Russian cosmonaut, remarked that having been into deep space, he had not seen God anywhere…

"Moshe reached out with his staff toward the sky and Adonai sent thunder and hail and fire (lightning) ran down to the earth. Adonai caused it to hail on the land of Egypt… but in the land of Goshen where the people of Israel were, there was no hail."
Exodus 9:24-26 (CJB)

"Joshua said to the Lord in the presence of Israel: O sun stand still over Gibeon, O moon over the Valley of Aijalon. So the sun stood still and the moon stopped till the nation avenged itself on its enemies."
Joshua 10:12-13

"He makes the clouds His chariot and rides on the wings of the wind."
Psalm 104:3

Wings of the Wind

Who can understand it,
who can tame its will ?
Has anyone ever seen the wind?

Can you sit on a cloud,
jump and gambol in its billows?
Has anyone ever captured a cloud?

Who may calm the thunder,
hide from its mighty voice ?
Has anyone ever managed to turn it down?

Have you seen the lightning,
fork and sheet alike are blinding,
has anyone yet harnessed its power?

What of the fleeting moment?
Who may grasp its ephemeral pulse?
Has anyone ever stopped the march of time?

Has anyone here seen God yet,
talked to Him face to face,
made Him sit and listen to our 'plaint?

He who makes the clouds His chariot
and rides on the wings of the wind,
has anyone found out yet where He lives?

"Then Adonai, God, formed a person [Hebrew: adam] from the dust of the ground... Adonai, God, took the person and put him in the garden of Eden to cultivate and care for it..."
Genesis 2:7, 15 *(CJB)*

"He [God] never left Himself without a witness. There were always His reminders, such as sending you rain and good crops and giving you food and joyful hearts."
Acts 14:17 *(NLT)*

Glen Clova

Just walking along, on a day like spring
between the hills all purple with ling
our conversation halted by a sound!

That exquisite song of water tumbling
stirring the soul with gentle murm'ring,
we listened as the music echoed round.

Then searching around all the silent hills
for some gushing fount or rippling rills
naught could we see on all that purple ground.

We strolled on and on as the sound grew more
'til, guided by its crescending roar,
suddenly the wellspring had been found.

A small rivulet running down the Ben
reached the grassy edge of the hill, then
a tiny cataract to rocky bound.

We gasped at the beauty of what we saw,
a rippling pool made by nature's law,
with flowers, ferns and grasses all around.

No master-gard'ner could ever have planned
a lovelier feature in wild land,
this perfectly formed garden and its sound.

We stood to praise the great God who had made
such a place that e'en in mountain's shade
could make its beauty in our hearts redound.

"God has made everything beautiful for its own time. He has planted eternity in the human heart, but even so, people cannot see the whole scope of God's work from beginning to end."
Ecclesiastes 3:11 *(NLT)*

Wishing I Could Paint...

I wished so hard that I could paint,
as I walked beside the river on the way.
Gulls were diving, crying, swooping
and the water gurgling, rushing
as I walked along the river path that day.

Oh! I wished so hard that I could paint,
for the sun was warm and people laughed that day.
Children's voices, distant barking,
wispy clouds high up above us
as I stood and loved this scene of life that day.

I wished that I could share thro' paint
the beauty and vitality of the day,
with brush strokes for the colour and the movement -
but the sounds! How would I tell
what they'd added by their music constantly?

So, I thanked the God of Heaven above
for the scenes and sounds He'd given me all the way.
Then I took a piece of paper
and a pen so I could write
this poem, to share the symphony of that day.

"...remember... how I carried you on eagle's wings and brought you to myself."
Exodus 19:4 (CJB)

"He forgives all your offences. He heals all your diseases. He redeems your life from the pit. He surrounds you with grace and compassion. He contents you with good as long as you live so that your youth is renewed like an eagle's."
Psalm 103:3-5

What Do You Want Me To Do?

In Beit-Zata was a healing pool
where the blind and crippled lay.
One man had been there thirty-eight years
just waiting, day after long day.

Then Yeshua came by and asked him:
"What is it you want?" The man said
"I want to get into the water
be rid of this sickness and bed."

"Rise up and walk," the Stranger replied.
The man did, and suddenly knew
he could no longer a beggar be,
he'd stand on his own feet, made new.

We're not told much more of his story,
set free from all sin, its pain too.
We're each asked the very same question:
"What do you want Me to do?"

We can live life without the tangles
of sin, the insidious lie
that keeps us in darkness and turmoil
when God wants to teach us to fly.

Come on! Learn to fly. He is off'ring
the same thing to you as to me.
Don't waste any more time just waiting;
Yeshua will teach you, you'll see.

CS Lewis once commented that people tended to think of 'holiness' as dull until they met with the real thing, then they found it irresistible.

"And a main road will go through that once deserted land. It will be named the Highway of Holiness... Those who have been ransomed by the Lord will return to Jerusalem singing songs of everlasting joy. Sorrow and mourning will disappear and they will be overcome with joy and gladness."
Isaiah 35:8, 10 (NLT

Irresistible

To meet an outcast woman
with rock-bottom self-esteem
and lift her to a place of confidence
so she could now meet others
face aglow and eyes agleam
and tell them: "Life' s diff'rent now"-
that's Holiness.

To take a man born sightless
from the darkness of his soul
and make his eyes to work, his mind to see
that he had worth in God's eyes
and work now that he could do
to tell how he'd been freed –
that's Holiness.

To take a boy with demons
plagued with water, sometimes fire,
and set this trapped young man at liberty
from powers that were running rife,
return him to his parents
now free to enter life–
that's Holiness.

To hang in execution
put there by those you'd healed
with sorrow for their blindness and the sin
that, through anger, hate and lust
makes each one less than MAN,
and ask, "Father forgive …" –
that's Holiness.

"…Think about the fields of wild irises, and how they grow. They neither work nor spin thread, yet I tell you that not even Shlomo [Solomon] in all his glory was clothed as beautifully as one of these."
Matthew 6:28-29 *(CJB)*

Hope Springs...

A crowded train
people like sardines
the end of the working day.
Trains rushing thro'
stations and marsh'lling yards
bleak sightings along the way
of blocks of flats and washing
graffiti on fences and walls.
Train stops in dismal outpost
workmen in overalls.
Faces are glum, impassive
when through the window appears
the sight of a buddleia growing
between lines, expelling all fears
that there is, in this life, any situation without hope.

"With the hand of Adonai upon me, Adonai carried me out by his Spirit and set me down in the middle of the valley, and it was full of bones... and they were so dry! He asked me: 'Human being, can these bones live?' I answered: 'Adonai Elohim! Only you know that!'"
***Ezekiel 37:1-3** (CJB)*

"There is hope of a tree, if it be cut down, that it will sprout again and that the tender branch thereof will not cease."
***Job 14: 7** (KJV)*

Can These Bones Live?

In the vale of dry bones
where hope was gone,
You spoke and life returned.
I cannot comprehend,
but feel its certainty.

In the vale of dried life,
once known and loved
the young, who took the stuff
that alters minds,
then died to all reality.

In the vale of hard hearts
once full of expectation,
dashed by hurts common to man,
now in self-made cells
of false security.

You speak and life returns.
Our hope revives!
You who are the Word of life
I pray You speak.
Restore that lost vitality.

"As the sparrow finds herself a home, and the swallow her nest, where she lays her young, so my resting place is by your altars, Adonai, my king and my God."
Psalm 84:4{3} (CJB)

"Aren't sparrows sold for next to nothing... yet not one of them will fall to the ground without your Father's consent. As for you, every hair of your head has been counted. So do not be afraid, you are worth more than many sparrows."
Matthew 10:29-30

Risky Business

I wondered where they all had gone
on days when snow lay thickly on the ground.
Sparrows, bluetits, finches, robin, blackbirds,
well, they were simply nowhere to be found.

Breadcrumbs buried in deepest snow
the water in the birdbath turned to ice
I really missed those birds from round the garden
and hoped winter would soon release its vice.

Then I spotted it on the wall
its size and shape outlined against the sky,
the sparrow-hawk had surely come to call!
I prayed those little birds were still snow-shy.

When the snow finally melted
seeds, nuts and crumbs were all put out again
the birds were back to play and eat and fly
that meant the hawk had hunted here in vain.

The birds were really up against it
while snow and hawk made life a risky sphere.
They could not escape from this life's dangers,
they just laid low, and joy of joy they're here.

"We escaped like a bird from a hunter's trap. The trap is broken and we are free."
Psalm 124:7 *(NLT)*

"For He will rescue you from every trap…"
Psalm 91:3

Born to Fly

The fowler set his snare to trap the bird
and for a time the bird was caught in there,
but someone came along and saw his plight
he loosed the catch, the bird soared free in air.

Like birds we too were caught to fly no more.
So many snares had tripped and held us fast,
but Someone came along and saw our plight.
He loosed each catch and cancelled all the past.

So many 'birds' now fly who once were trapped.
They soar and sing, relishing all they see,
while others sit in snares, catches broken
and die there, never knowing they've been freed.

There's no snare Yeshua cannot loosen
no matter how, or when the bird was caught.
Don't be scared to fly to Him in freedom!
For you may surely trust in all He taught.

Born to fly, don't let the snares of this world
rob you of the life He came to give.
Take it with both hands and trust the Giver.
In this freedom we're always meant to live.

" Then the Lord gave me this message, 'Oh Israel, can I not do with you as this potter has done with his clay? As the clay is in the potter's hand so are you in my hand.'"
Jeremiah 18:1-6 (NLT)

"…because those whom He knew in advance, He also determined in advance would be conformed to the pattern of His Son, so that He might be the firstborn among many brothers [and sisters]."
Romans 8:29 (CJB)

Supreme Potter

Thrown on to the Great Potter's wheel,
just a sad, helpless lump of clay
moving thro' those skilful, firm hands
as He works to mould it His Way.
Beginning to form the vessel
that in His mind's eye He can see
the patient Artisan works on
to make what He wants it to be.

Alas! Those masterful fingers
find a hardness that will not yield.
Living water moistens the clay,
He replaces it on His wheel.
Never will He resign His work,
nor ever will cast it away
'til each vessel is formed complete,
He'll rework it 'til that great Day
when all the vessels He has made
stand upright in that mighty throng,
where those once hopeless lumps of clay,
now glorify Him with their song.

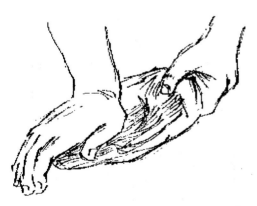

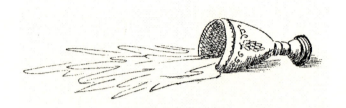

"It [wine] may glide down smoothly now but in the end, it bites like a serpent – yes, it strikes like a poisonous snake."
Proverbs 23:31-32 *(CJB)*

"The sting of death is sin; and sin draws its power from the Torah (God's counsel) but thanks be to God, who gives us the victory through our Lord Yeshua the Messiah!"
1 Corinthians 15:36-37

the sting

few people want to think that we're all sinners
we protest our innocence loud and clear
"i've never murdered, stolen, hurt another
i really care"

we think that God must be a fuddy-duddy
we cannot help our weakness, don't say sin
we know one day we'll die, but not today, Sir!
pray have no fear

"sin is the sting of death" so God's word tells us
He says this body it will surely die
but spirit living in us goes on living
do you know where?

sin's not so much our deeds as our condition
each man's child born with this *sting* in the heel
each under grace 'til' choice becomes our due, friend
have you made yours?

the pay for being mortal must be death but
eternal spirit must in some state be
the ways of death and life both lie before us
choose life, it's free

satan is a spirit who's defeated now
he'll live on then in everlasting fire
will you be joining him in hopeless exile?
God is not there

Yeshua pulled the sting at resurrection
so when this body dies i know that i
will live with God our Father in pure glory
will you be there?

the life HE offers us begins in this world!
it's not just for eternity alone
we learn all things to face with Him o'ercoming
on our way home.

"For God so loved the world that He gave His only Son so that everyone who believes in Him will not perish but have eternal life. God did not send His Son into the world to condemn it, but to save it."
John 3:16-17 (NLT)

"When the Son of Man comes in his glory…he will sit on his glorious throne. All the nations will be assembled before him, and he will separate people one from another as a shepherd separates sheep from goats. The 'sheep' he will place at his right hand but the 'goats' at his left."
Matthew 25:31-33 (CJB)

The Scarlet Thread

"It's the battle between good and evil!"
That's what the people all say.
"Good on the right and evil on the left!
Choose which you'll fight for today."

But that's not the real truth of this battle.
It's not what God has to say.
"Sheep on the right and the goats on the left.
Choose whom you'll follow today."

All the good that we would do, we do not,
evil we wouldn't we do!
To be on the right and not on the left
you make that choice, only you

One strand of this thread is our scarlet sin,
the other, rescue thro' blood.
saved on the right the unsaved on the left,
for God knows only His good

God has told us He looks on our heart-set.
We see appearance alone.
New hearts on the right, old hearts on the left,
choose Christ, who for all did atone.

"Is my arm too short to redeem? Have I too little power to save?"
"…Adonai Elohim has given me the ability to speak as a man well taught,
so that I…know how to sustain the weary."
***Isaiah 50:4** (CJB)*

The Old Testament is full of wonderful faulty people just like us and this poem is about
*some of them. We meet the people from this poem in the Books of **Genesis**, **Exodus**, **Joshua**, and **Esther**, also in the genealogy of the Lord Yeshua the Messiah in **Matthew's Gospel** and in **Hebrews 11**.*

Warts and All

I love to read of Abraham and Isaac
Jacob, Joseph, Moses,
Rahab and Esther, and the rest.
All God's servants who, like me
were Oh! so very imperfect.

I love to read of how my God
changed these imperfect folks,
endued them with His Spirit
and drew them to Himself.

The centre of His vision, they
obeyed the God of Heaven and
pioneered the way thro' this dark place
of man's greed and lust for control.

Who am I? Another frail imperfect being
with a mighty Heavenly Father.
I look back, not with longing but relief
and wonder:
"How does it come about
that I'm still here?"

"By my God I can leap over a wall"
the Psalmist said.
"Not I but Christ living in me"
is my response.
Thus we agree.

"So Bil'am [Balaam] got up in the morning, saddled his donkey and went with the princes of Mo'av. But God's anger flared up because he went and the angel of Adonai stationed himself on the path to bar his way... The angel of Adonai said to him: 'Why did you hit your donkey three times like that? I have come out here to bar your way because you are rushing to oppose me. The donkey saw me and turned aside... if she had not turned aside I would have killed you by now and saved it alive.'"
Numbers 22:2, 22, 32-33 (CJB)

"Shimshon [Samson] said: 'With the jawbone of a donkey I left heaps piled on heaps!
With the jawbone of a donkey I killed a thousand men!'"
Judges 15:16

"Say to the daughter of Tziyon, 'Look! Your King is coming to you, riding humbly on a donkey, and on a colt, the offspring of a beast of burden!'"
Zechariah 9:9, quoted in Matthew 21:4

Ode To the Donkey

Tamed and broken ass to which we owe
so much esteem.
Our little beast of burden, uncomplaining
working hard
that mankind's lot might be eased,
from Balaam's encounter with death,
he the obstinate one
not you who saved his life,
to Samson's triumph over those
who wished him dead.
You already were, yet your jawbone
was the weapon he required.
Your greatest hours were when
you carried Him, first while still unborn,
to the humble stable you knew as home.
Indeed any clump of hay sufficed
for you - and Him.
That cross shape on your back!
Can it be
the Creator's mark to show that He
who sat on you once more to ride
into the jaws of death
hung there Himself, broken and dead
to rise again
that I might live?

"Again I observed all the oppression that takes place in our world: I saw the tears of the oppressed with no-one to comfort them. The oppressors have great power and the victims are helpless."
Ecclesiastes 4:1 (NLT)

"The sun will be turned to darkness... before the great and terrible day of the Lord comes."
Acts 2:20, quoting Joel 2:28-32

"...a voice from the cloud said, "This is my SON, whom I love: with Him I am well pleased. Listen to HIM."
Matthew 17:5 (NKJV)

Note:

Haiku and Senryu are Japanese verse forms in three lines with 5 – 7 – 5 syllables respectively, as in the manner of this poem. Haikus generally are concerned with the natural, while Senryus concern human affairs.

The Light

Sun streams thro' window
dust atoms fly everywhere
not seen without sun.

Earth's air's polluted
Sin's effects are everywhere
not seen without SON.

"On that day, many will say to me, 'Lord, Lord! Didn't we prophesy in your name? Didn't we perform many miracles in your name?' Then I will tell them to their faces, 'I never knew you.'"
***Matthew 7:22-23** (CJB)*

"The religious observance that God the Father considers pure and faultless is this: to care for orphans and widows in their distress and to keep oneself from being contaminated by the world."
James 1:27

*Continuing the theme of sin's effects being everywhere, **The Jute Mill** has a change of rhythm in stanzas 6 and 7 to represent the different tenor of lives lived with plenty but carelessly.*

The Jute Mill

Noisy, thunderous roar of those looms
and the spinning machines for jute.
Women in pinnies, the dust in their lungs
while the owners all counted their loot.

Each morning at six, the claxon call
told the women 'twas time for t'mill,
where they'd grind 'til two in the afternoon,
then go home and clean house with a will,

and with cut hands where the merciless jute
hacked deep through their hardening skin,
cleaned and cooked such food as there was
and enjoyed what they could with their kin.

Exhausted, tired out they'd fall into bed
where husband expected admittance,
and wished it was Friday so they'd collect
small wage, we call it a pittance.

The following week they would start at two
and finish quite late at eleven.
Red-eyed and gaunt they'd run home to see
their children in beds without linen.

The mill owners now, on the other hand,
built themselves villas on the choicest land.
Their offspring went to the very best schools
and all were dressed in the best silks and wools.

continued...

They sat down at table to eat the best food,
young lives favoured with all that seemed good
except to respect those who worked in the mill,
such goodness seldom was seen in their will.

No matter! Mill women received their lot.
In their lives they had dealt with much death
of children and husbands and friends from t'mill,
the survivors themselves, most went deaf.

The jute it was used for various things
like sacking, lino and carpet backing.
Things that were needed by wealthy folks,
the cost was heavy and pity lacking

I wonder what happened when they all died
and faced the Great Judge from on high?
He who knows the deep essence of 'good'
and in whom there's no darkness or lie.

"Just as you've done either ill or good
to one of the least of my brethern,
you've done it to Me," said the Judge of all,
He who sits on the great throne in Heaven.

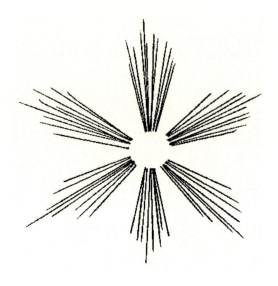

"For with You is the fountain of life; in Your light we see light."
Psalm 36:10 (CJB)

"Your Word is a lamp for my foot
and light on my path."
Psalm 119:105

Window

God's Word like window
Darkness takes away our sight
window lets in light.

"He debated with himself, 'What shall I do? I haven't enough room for all my crops.' Then he said, '...I'll tear down all my barns and build bigger ones... Then I'll say... Eat! Drink! Enjoy yourself!' But God said 'You fool! This very night you will die...'"
Luke 12:17-20 *(CJB)*

"Yeshua said to him, 'If you are serious about reaching the goal, go and sell your possessions, give to the poor, and you will have riches in heaven.' But when the young man heard this, he went away sad because he was wealthy."
Matthew 19:21-22

The Great Caricature

The Gospel of Yeshua is, "God loves YOU"
and that's easy to believe when we see HIM,
but the Church so often tells a diff'rent story
by the lives of those who dare to claim His Name.

The selfless, servant life of the Messiah
binding broken hearts and healing bodies sore,
stood in contrast to the pious, robed professors
as they marketed religion from their lore.

Like many folks of old we seem to think that
it's about acquiring land here on the earth.
Houses, cars, and schools, with fine clothes of distinction
as we sit to hear great sermons of such worth!

When we're asked to give more than just a 'gesture'
we ask, "Will that be before or after tax?"
We're afraid that moving out will bring disaster
so we hang on to the old ruts just in case.

The message of the Gospel's not about land!
It's about the love of GOD for every one
Not about inheritance or wealth in this world
but family through the Father's only SON.

Many earthquakes, floods, famines and tsunamis
surely teach us that we don't control the land.
It can be taken from us so don't die for it
for your future will be safe in Father's hand.

Let the single, widow, orphan and outcast
come inside our corp'rate life to feel the warmth
of love abounding, where God is at the centre
of the life of people trav'lling through His earth.

"For this reason, I fall on my knees before the Father, from whom every family in heaven and on earth receives its character."
Ephesians 3:14-15 *(CJB)*

"Moreover, an attacker may defeat someone who is alone, but two can resist him; and a three-stranded cord is not easily broken."
Ecclesiastes 4:12

The poem opposite was written when I saw this scene in an old movie and felt momentary nostalgia, not for what I once had because, like so many, I did not, but for what God had intended for everyone.
"...love covers all offences..." *Proverbs 10:12 (NLT)*

The Nuclear Family

In the family disagreement
all went their separate ways
appetites gone they left their cake;
angry, sad and disunited they
went to their rooms to cry, wail
feel sorry and lost, or to pray.

Father and Mother had
disagreed with each other,
Father adamant and Mother
unhappy with his decision,
each child felt threatened and
took to their own safe cells,
while the house fell silent.

Father despondent – he only wanted
the best for each child and his wife.
She loved him and hated to see
him cast down so in life.
She went to him with assurance
that she knew that he knew
what he was doing.

While he ate his cake,
Mother went to the piano
and began to play a
familiar, romantic song.
Father joined in and
they sang together.
Gradually, one by one,
the children left their rooms,
each took a piece of cake then
sat down to eat and talk
with each other.

continued…

The nucleus had not split but
was strengthened so that
the membrane of the family
remained and was safe.
Troubles would still be
but their love was strong
enough.

"A Father of the fatherless, defender of widows is God in His holy dwelling. God sets the solitary in families, He sets prisoners free and gives them joy."
Psalm 68:5-6 (paraphrase)

IDENTITY

What's it all about, Lord?

"It's about people – people who are lost, child."

How are they lost, my Father?
I'm lost – I feel lost
But I can't explain it – except
It's like hunger, a hunger to belong
To someone who is not changing and transient.

One day my Mother will die…
What will I do when she is dead?
Where will be my identity?

My earthly father left us
So there's no identity there.
You set the solitary in families but
Nuclear fission has set in there
So where
is our identity?

"It is in Me, child.
I made you for myself.
The hunger in you is
your yearning for the Eternal…

I AM that I AM.
Come unto Me."

"When Avram [Abraham] was 99 years old Adonai appeared to Avram and said to him, 'I am El Shaddai (God Almighty). Walk in my presence and be pure-hearted. I will make my covenant between me and you, and I will increase your numbers greatly... As for me this is my covenant with you: you will be the father of many nations. I will cause you to be very fruitful. I will make nations of you. Kings will descend from you.'"
Genesis 17:1-4, 6 *(CJB)*

"This is the genealogy of Yeshua the Messiah, son of David, son of Avraham..."
Matthew 1:1

"Be assured then, that it is those who live by trusting and being faithful who are really children of Avraham...So, then those who rely on trusting and being faithful are blessed along with Avraham, who trusted and was faithful."
Galatians 3:6, 9

How Do I Know?

How do I know da Vinci lived?
Or Beethoven or Napoleon?
I see, hear or read of their works
but know no-one who met them.

How do I know Christ Jesus lives?
I am His work and
live my days at peace with His creation.
His voice renews my mind with God's perspective.
From Genesis to Revelation I may read of Him.

As for those who have met Him,
they are numerous as the sands of the sea
and span the whole of history.
I'm part of the largest family, ever.

The story in this poem is found in the Book of Numbers, Chapters 27 and 36. Its veracity and integrity are followed thro' in the New Testament as we see Yeshua according equal dignity to women and men.

"The blessing of the Lord makes us rich and adds no sorrow with it." So says King Solomon in **Proverbs 10:22**. (NKJV)

The Father's Children

A man from the tribe of Manasseh died,
five daughters were left behind.
There was not a son to carry his name thro' the lines of humankind.

Now five daughters could not inherit as
such had never arisen
but the five came to Moshe with spirit, "Give us our rights for living."

So Moshe consulted with Adonai,
the answer came back right away,
"The daughters must have their inheritance; proclaim this my law today."

The girls were glad for their God had now shown
that His love and His law were fair.
Provision was thus a God-given right, like sons they would have their
share.

Now, later on a real problem arose
as the daughters grew and were fair.
Other tribes too had handsome men who might take them as wives with
their share.

So, the men of the tribe of Manasseh
came to Moshe once more, "Please guide!
If our women should wed those men, they'll inherit the land of our tribe."

"Not so," was the answer God gave to this.
"With rights come responsibility!
The daughters must marry men from their tribe – that's tribal fidelity."

continued…

They did this gladly, so all was preserved
through God-given laws that are just.
The blessing of God that made each one rich with no anger, greed or lust.

This truth is clear and exists for us all.
It's from God that our rights must come.
He alone knows what is good and right and He treats each one as His
son.

With God there is neither Jew nor Gentile,
neither male or female either
All are one and treated as one, for each is a child of the Father.

*"With your ears you will hear a word from behind you: 'This is the way;
stay on it, whether you go to the right or the left.'"*
Isaiah 30:21(CJB)

*"Examine me, God, and know my heart; test me, and know my thoughts.
See if there is in me any hurtful way, and lead me along the eternal way."*
Psalm 139:23-24

*"Trust in Adonai with all your heart; do not rely on your own
understanding. In all your ways acknowledge Him; then He will level
your paths."*
Proverbs 3:5-6

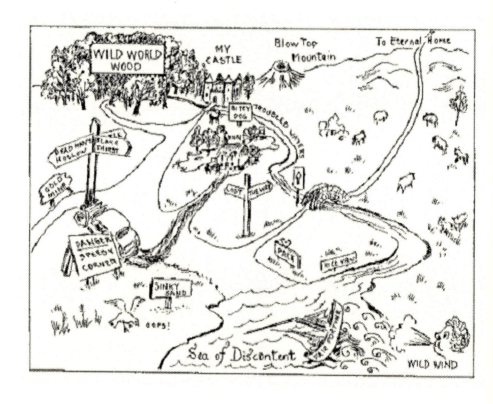

Wild World Navigation Map

I asked God for many things
that I thought would make me glad.
When, thro' time I had them all
they also made me sad.

I asked God, "Why is this so?"
for I did not understand.
He leaned down to hear my cry
then took me by the hand,

He led me thro' all life's storms,
at times my heart was broken.
"You see child, the world is wild
but your Way through bespoken
by My Son's sacrifice for you
that you may overcome
to the last enemy of death
and reach Eternal Home."

I thank God for each new day
knowing now that He will show
which of all the paths in life
is that on which I'll go.

I ask Him for nothing more
than to be with me each day
I do not fear this wild world
knowing He is the Way.

"How blessed is the man who trusts in Adonai and does not look to the arrogant or to those who rely on things that are false."
Psalm 40: 5 *(CJB)*

The story of Naomi and Ruth is told in the **Book of Ruth** *in the* **Old Testament***. Ruth is also mentioned in the genealogy of Yeshua in Matthew's account of the Gospel,*
Matthew 1:5*.*

The Real Book of Ruth

Elimelekh ran to a Gentile land,
he did not now trust in his God.
When famine came he took all things in hand
and went with his kin to find food.

Some years in Moab, his sons all grown up
he married them off and felt pleased
to think of the grandsons who'd share his cup,
and how all their lives had been eased.
Alas!
Elimelekh died and so did his sons
without issue, his line did end.
Naomi, his widow, was now alone
with daughters-in-law in strange land.

She made a decision that showed her brave
to return to God and her land,
the land of Judea where she could have
her faith back through trust in God's hand.

Orpah said, "Now, I cannot come with you.
I must stay and the journey is long."
While Ruth said, "Your God will be my God too
and I'll live there and learn your song."

The journey from Moab, near fifty miles
on foot, was hard. They felt alone
but God kept them safe, they arrived with smiles
when they reached the land now their home.

continued…

Ruth's story from there is of course well known,
Rahab's daughter-in-law she became.
So, God had seen that the seed He'd long sown
established the line of His reign.

King David, Solomon and the others
they all came along in due course
'Til Yeshua called sisters and brothers
by the Good News of God's free saving grace.

This is no rosy story of glitter and glow!
From error and hardship it grew.
Elimelekh died and God's works seemed slow
tho' His purposes real and true.

If you would serve God in this alien world
Don't settle for safety and friends.
Step into the cold and see what He'll do
when He applies your weak faith to His ends.

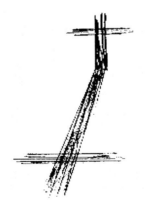

"But while he was still a long way off, his father saw him...He ran and threw his arms around him and kissed him warmly. His son said to him, 'Father, I have sinned...' but his father said to his slaves 'Quick, bring out a robe, the best one..."
Luke 15: 20-22 *(CJB)*

*The parable of the Prodigal Son is told in the Gospel account by Luke, in the New Testament, starting at **Luke 15:11**.*

Prodigal

Prodigal leaves home
wastes years, money, health to rove
Returns to find love.

Maybe home's not good
runs feeling lost and alone
God's Kingdom's good, come.

Father loves lost child
No anger, or payment due
Waits, watches for you.

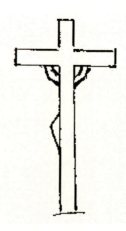

" I will not fail nor forsake you..."
Joshua 1:5, quoted in Hebrews 13:5 (KJV)

"Why have you forsaken me?"
Psalm 22:1, quoted in Matthew 27:46 and Mark 15:34

"...lo! I am with you always, even to the end of the age."
Matthew 28:20

Forsaken

One place on this earth
ever was 'God-forsaken,'
Calvary alone.

"All creation anticipates the day when it will join God's children in glorious freedom from death and decay. For we know that all creation has been groaning as in the pains of childbirth right up to the present time."
Romans 8:21-22 (NLT)

A Diamonte is a poem in the shape of a diamond.
It moves from the subject at the top to a different, maybe opposite subject at the bottom.

The route:
Line 1: Noun (subject 1)
Line 2: Two adjectives describing subject 1
Line 3: Three participles ending in 'ing,' telling about subject 1
Line 4: Four nouns – 2 relate to subject 1 and 2 relate to subject 2
Line 5: Three participles, ending in 'ing,' about subject 2
Line 6: Two adjectives describing subject 2
Line 7: Noun (subject 2)

Last Word

Creation
beautiful desecrated
living groaning waiting
Earth life humanity GOD
winnowing rewarding avenging
terrible retributory
Judgement.

"'And to every wild animal, bird in the air and creature crawling on the earth, in which there is a living soul, I am giving as food every kind of green plant.' And that is how it was. God saw everything that he had made, and indeed it was very good."

Genesis 1:30-31 (NLT)

The Heron

Consider him stately in the river,
one leg angled 'gainst the other.
Motionless he stands as reeds all quiver,
camouflaged and still in coolest water.

Unsuspecting fish swims past,
he waits until it's close and still,
then his head stoops and quick as a flash
the piscene swim ends in his bill.

Clever bird!!

"Then God said, 'Let us make people in our own image, to be like ourselves. They will be masters over all life...' So God created people in His own image, God patterned them after Himself, male and female created He them."
Genesis 1:26-27 (NLT)

"And the Lord God formed a man's body from the dust of the ground and breathed into it the breath of life. And the man became a living person."
Genesis 2:7

"The wolf will lie down with the lamb, the leopard lie down with the kid: calf, young lion and lamb together, with a little child to lead them..."
Isaiah 11:6 (CJB)

"Then Jesus came out wearing the crown of thorns and the purple robe. And Pilate said 'Ecce Homo!'" [Behold the Man!]
John 19:5 (NLT)

ECCE HOMO

I love animals, I truly do
and the young of every species
is beautiful

but I am not one, not an ape
of higher order or species
homo erectus.

there's no missing link, man is unique
essentially made corpus et spiritus
mortal and immortal

for God breathed His Life into man
while beasts He created and animated
corpus alone.

all flesh must die for sin corrupts all
but spirit immortal lives on
in heaven or hell.

while "all things made new" means animals too
"the wolf will lie down with the lamb"
in the new Earth

my spirit in Christ will be there
He pulled out the sting of my death
so in Him I will rise

to life eternal new creation
where nothing will ever again die.
ECCE HOMO!

"If I raise my eyes to the hills, from where will my help come?
My help comes from Adonai, the maker of heaven and earth."
Psalm 121:1

IMAGINE IF...

Imagine if Christ had never lived!
Had never preached the Sermon on the Mount;
Told nothing of Samaritan, Prodigal or Sower's seed;
No word of the Father's love, joy, peace – no fount
of grace to help in time of need.
Lame, deaf or blind – he could not save;
Never called Zaccheus from the tree;
no raising of child or Lazarus from the grave;
no pardon to offer either you or me.
Imagine! if Christ had never lived.

Imagine if Christ had never died!
No heat or bloody sweat in dark Gethsemane,
Nor prayer that only His Father's will be done;
No price ever paid to ransom you or me;
No crown of life, for death itself had won.
No Calvary's cost, no bitter wormwood or gall;
The soldier's sword did find no side to pierce;
No women weeping in that deadly pall
While blind mankind regaled with mocking fierce.
Imagine! if Christ had never died.

Imagine if Christ had never risen!
No empty tomb to witness on that Sabbath morn,
Nor joyous cry escape on Mary's part;
No temple curtain rift, in two parts torn
Making free passage to the Father's heart.
Meeting with no disciples in the morning's spell
With breakfast cooked upon the shore,
He gave no commission to – "Go and tell...
Peace with God and life for evermore."
Imagine! if Christ had never risen.

continued...

Imagine if His Spirit had not come!
No second chance for Peter's coward heart
To beat with newfound life and nerve;
For Saul to vent his spleen then change
To Paul and learn to serve.
No Church to rise from the ashes of human wills;
Lives lived despairingly, no hope to see;
All of us prisoners in our self-made cells
With no Redeemer who holds the key.
Imagine! if His Spirit had not come.

Imagine if the Gospel is simply true!
That Jesus lives and teaches how to live;
Offers to you and me His life in all its fullness clear,
His strength for us – "To you I freely give…
No longer must you walk in darkness or in fear.
The way to God is open and all His grace is free.
I call you now to come that I may wash you clean,
Lead you in the path of heavenly liberty
That you may know my life power, and on me lean."
Imagine! if the Gospel is simply true.

continued…

Imagine if I have been forgiven!
He lived! He died! He rose again and now
His Spirit lives within to show to me
How I may serve my God, by serving here below
My neighbour, whoever that may be?
What I am in human terms, loser, prisoner or slave,
great success, star or millionaire or king.
He measures not in what I am or have
He calls me too, from the grave and makes me sing.
Imagine! if I have been forgiven.

Imagine Christ had never lived?
Imagine Christ had never died?
Imagine Christ had never risen?
Imagine His spirit had never come?
Reality forbids.

"See, I have inscribed you on the palms of my hand."
Isaiah 49:16 (NKJV)

"Take two onyx stones and engrave on them the names of the tribes of Israel... Aaron will carry these names before the Lord as a constant reminder."
Exodus 28:9, 12 (NLT)

"Don't be afraid for I have redeemed you, I have called you by name..."
Isaiah 43:1

"...He calls His own sheep by name and leads them out."
John 10:3

He Knows Your Name

Faceless in the Underground or mall,
just another body in the mass,
"No-one really sees me, and no-one cares…"
We may feel this way as others pass.

"Why do people all have purpose,
look as tho' they know just where to go,
while I feel like an accident that happened
try to see despair and angst don't show?"

Yeshua said, "Mary." She saw Him
as she heard her name called thro' her tears
One of His ransomed, He showed His hands,
where He'd graven e'en her in those scars,

like th'onyx stones carried by Aaron,
engraved with the names of Israel's sons,
before Adonai God who'd commanded
that this most sacred thing must be done.

When we feel ourselves lost in the mass,
we may settle for despair's domain
or recall the price paid for our ransom,
His Word says, "I have called YOU by name."

"He will feed His flock like a shepherd. He will carry the lambs in His arms, holding them close to His heart. He will gently lead the mother sheep with their young."

Isaiah 40:1 (NLT)

The Lamb

It sat upon its mother's back
as she rested in the field.
It nestled in the hollow
that her posture prone did yield,
and as she lay on grasses green,
her breathing rose and fell.
The lamb was sitting all serene
as they undulated well.
We marvelled at this pastoral calm
and passing, turned again
to see that by her other side
another lamb was lain.
The three paid no attention
to our close proximity,
all settled as they were
in warm tranquility.

The poem opposite is based on the story of King David as it is told in
2 Samuel 11-12 *and* **Psalm 51,**
and on **Galatians 6.**

WHEN THE LIGHT IN US IS DARKNESS

King David was a chosen man, the apple of God's eye,
but when 'forbidden fruit' he saw, it caused his heart to lie.
While walking on his palace roof because he could not sleep
he saw the fair Bathsheba bathe and covertly did peep.

So, darkness came to him that night, presenting just like
light,
he was convinced it was not wrong to relish now this sight
of beautiful Bathsheba – wife of soldier brave and strong.
David had not sought out this chance, how could it then be
wrong?

The King, he did not turn away while time was still his
friend,
he started on a bitter path not knowing where 'twould end,
nor who might be the victims in the web he started then,
he exercised his pow'r and brought Bathsheba to his den.

Forgetting the Creator had put laws at Nature's heart,
the furtive pair then satisfied their lust and, shrewd, did
part.
Believing sin is only sin if it's known you have erred,
the pair continued with their lives, by God's law undeterred.

until, in time Bathsheba found a babe was there inside.
She panicked, knowing that in time a child is hard to hide
from husband who has been away too long to now believe
it was himself who with his wife this blessing did conceive.

continued…

And when Uriah David tried to push to wedlock pleasure,
he found that of this noble man he had not quite the
measure.
"The men of battle lie in tents and hardship is their life!
Shall I, Commander, priv'lege take and go home to my wife?

Not so," Uriah cried, and so a warrant must be signed,
such honor meant that to the Front Uriah be assigned.
There in a battle glorious, the soldier brave would die,
covered in glory and honour the slain hero would lie!

Who could know why his death contrived in this manner
had been?
The night of adult'ry was dark, only themselves had seen.
The King then wed Bathsheba, the babe was born in due
course,
but prophet Nathan came to reveal this dark error's source.

The events of that night in the dark, had begun a train
of ruin and sorrow and sadness, making life seem vain.
The King, distraught with grief when the baby boy was
taken
to Heaven to live with God, earthly parents forsaken,

knelt and bowed low his head and for his God's mercy he
sighed,
"I recognise my shameful deeds, they haunt me," David
cried.
"'Tis Uriah I have killed. I had him put to the sword,
but it is against You I have sinned, I have spurned Your
Word.

continued...

88

And the pain of heart is so great I can scarce lift my head,
Bathsheba I married, now my innocent child is dead.
Teach me to walk to the beat of Your heart, this now I pray,
Then to other sinners, I pledge I'll live to teach Your Way."

How clever we are at believing that evil is good.
Neither thought they'd cover their sin with a man's noble
blood!
But God is not mocked, His Word tells us to walk in His
Light.
To love and do good unto *all* – that is 'good' in His sight.

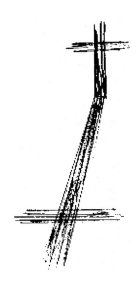

"God said, "Let the water swarm with swarms of living creatures, and let birds fly above the earth in the open dome of the sky. " …the water swarmed with all kinds of them and there was every kind of winged bird: and God saw that it was good. Then God blessed them, saying, "Be fruitful and multiply and fill the water of the sea…"
Genesis 1:20 (CJB)

"The fear and dread of you will be upon every wild animal, every bird in the air, every creature populating the ground and all the fish in the sea; they have been handed over to you."
Genesis 9:2

View From a Bridge

As we stood there and watched from the bridge
the graceful bird glided towards us
detached from our world, almost unaware
of our presence or even existence,
and if she knew we were there at all
she cared not, for her task it was plain
she sailed to her nest beneath the curved span
and we saw there not a lone swan but twain.
The Pen on her journey maternal
on a mission she knew must not fail
her elegant neck, her movement so calm,
carried the cygnet she'd borne in her tail.
Like a ship with tall mast she carried her babe
all safe to the nest, and we left them to rest.

WHY?

"One day, when Joshua was there by Jericho, he raised his eyes and looked and in front of him stood a man with his sword drawn in his hand. 'Are you on our side or on the side of our enemies?'
'No' he replied, 'but I am the commander of Adonai's army.'... Joshua fell down with his face to the ground and worshipped him."
Joshua 5:13-14 *(CJB)*

"But I say love your enemies! Pray for those who persecute you! In that way you will be acting as true children of your Father in Heaven. For He gives His sunlight to both the evil and the good and He sends rain on the just and the unjust."
Matthew 5:44-45 *(NLT)*

WHY?

Why me? Why this? Why that? Why? Why?
I just want to know Lord God.
Why did You allow this cruel thing
that has caused us so much hurt?

Joshua asked the Man with the sword,
"Are you on my side or not?"
"I command the Lord's hosts" He said
"Are you on my side or not?"

So, it's not for us to question
what God in His world allows.
We must be sure to stand for Him
as He works for all to know

that His love for them has ransomed
each one who receives that blood
shed to redeem from death's dark vale
a stiff-necked, obstinate brood.

God wants truth in the inward parts
He will not settle for less.
Choose now today whom you'll follow,
stand with Him others to bless.

"Here on earth you will have many trials and sorrows. But take heart because I have overcome the world."
John 16:33

"A voice was heard in Ramah, sobbing and lamenting loudly. It was Rachel sobbing for her children and refusing to be comforted because they are no longer alive."
Matthew 2:18 *(CJB*

"Weeping may go on all night but joy comes with the morning."
Psalm 30:5 *(NLT)*

The Father's Will

I wonder if you've ever thought
of Moshe's Mum?
I wonder how it felt for her
to lose her son!

Moshe, he did not die of course
he lived right well,
while saved from Pharaoh's awful wrath
as prince to dwell.

She lost his boyhood years to find
another gained.
Jochabed's tears must flow and be,
her heart was pained.

Moshe was a man picked by God
to do His will.
His Mother would rejoice one day,
the bitter pill

would in time become life's lesson
about our kin.
tho' belonging to each other
it's first to HIM.

The Father gave His only Son
for us to kill.
I wonder how it felt for HIM?
It was His will.

Moshe set Israel's people free,
the Father willed,
asYeshua did for you and me.
God's Word fulfilled.

"Then children were brought to him so that He might lay His hands on them and pray for them, but the disciples rebuked the people bringing them. However, Yeshua said, 'Let the children come to me, don't stop them, for the Kingdom of Heaven belongs to such as these.'"
Matthew 19:13-14 *(CJB)*

"An infant will play on a cobra's hole, a toddler put his hand in a viper's nest. They will not hurt or destroy anywhere on my holy mountain, for the earth will be as full of the knowledge of Adonai as water covering the sea."
Isaiah 11:8-9

Eleanor

"She died when twenty-four hours old
and never knew this world.
Buried in a piece of ground
with strangers, in the cold."
My Mother told me this one day
tears tumbling in that place.
"I carried her for eight full months
and never saw her face."

Midwives took the babe away,
they said she'd not survive –
a time when babies premature
had little chance to live,
but cruellest blow of all
was yet to come to both.
My father 'drank' the burial fee
and wrapped the babe in cloth.

Placed in a stranger's burial box
to ground where poor or homeless lay,
my little sister, Eleanor's body
was finally taken away.

I found that 'Poor's Ground' recently
and planted there some flowers.
She's not there now, 'twas long ago
but the earth and the grass and the bowers
have something of my sister's essence
so I was glad to find that place,
give thanks to the God of Heaven
for knowledge of His saving grace.

A babe she entered thro' His gates
that eternally stand open
as a glorious welcome for all those
who leave this world as children.
God spared my Mother the awful pain
of seeing where her child's body lay.
They're in Heaven together now
rejoicing in eternal Day.

So thank you God my Father
that in Yeshua, Your Son,
over every evil of this sad place
the Victory has been won.

"Yes, indeed! I tell you that unless a grain of wheat that falls into the ground dies, it stays just a grain; but if it dies, it produces a big harvest."
John 12:24 *(CJB)*

"Continuing faithfully and with singleness of purpose to meet in the Temple courts daily, and breaking bread in their several homes, they shared their food in joy and simplicity of heart, praising God and having the respect of all the people. And day after day the Lord kept adding to them those who were being saved." **Acts 2:46-47**

Life from Death

Tiny corn of wheat
falls into the earth and dies
brings forth great harvest

God hangs on the Cross
to die and lie in dark tomb
Brings forth living Church

"God is our refuge and strength, an ever present help in trouble. Therefore we are unafraid, even if the earth gives way, even if the mountains tumble into the depths of the sea, even if its waters rage and foam, and mountains shake at its turbulence."

Psalm 46:2-4 *(CJB)*

"Adonai is my light and salvation; whom do I need to fear? Adonai is the stronghold of my life; of whom shall I be afraid?

Psalm 27:1

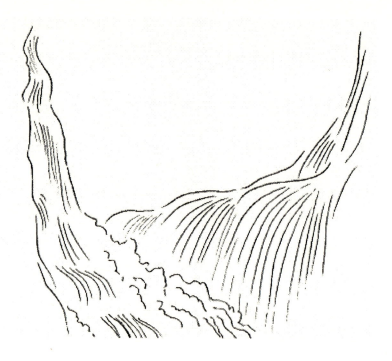

If I'd Been There...

When two school boys killed
a little boy in open air,
would it have been diff'rent
if I'd been there?
When some millions died
in the Holocaust over there,
would it have been diff'rent
if I'd been there?

When teacher despoiled
my child in empty classroom lair,
could it have been diff'rent
if I'd been there?
Would things be different
because another had been there?
You see, people were there
but were not aware.

Christ hung on the Cross
and many passed, seeing Him there
not knowing He made the diff'rence
by redeeming there.
Risen from that grave
from death's cold and merciless glare,
we may no diff'rence make,
but it's well – He's there.

"But his father said to the servants, 'Quick! Bring the finest robe in the house and put it on him…We must celebrate with a feast, for this son of mine was dead and has now returned to life. He was lost, but now he is found…'"
***Luke 15:22, 24** (NLT)*

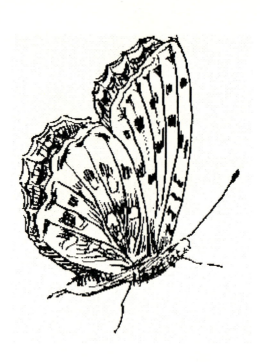

While He Was Gone

I had a boy-child, fifteen years old
sent him to school one day
unaware of evil waiting there
as the rugby coach laid a grim snare.

"Detention!" he shouted at my son.
Took him to a room where
he perpetrated an act on him,
left him to deal with his shock and fear.

Three times this happened in his fine school,
my son 'vanished' from view.
He would still come home from school each day
but behaviour changed, I knew

that my son was different and strange.
I asked others, they said,
"Now, don't worry! They're all just the same.
They go thro' such a phase. Rest your head."

For nine long years I then lost my son
ere I learned the grim tale.
Drugs, wrong-deeds, self-harm, need more be said?
He ran the full gamut wholesale!

continued…

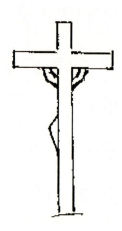

The 'hell' we lived in is over now.
God's grace has set him free
from years that the locusts have eaten
he is healed now and so he can 'be'.

"No anger now," he said
"I've learned things I would never have known."
His thought of others, his care for me,
how this whole human being has grown.

My son is home again,
my dear child died on that awful day.
It is a man who lives with me now.
He came here tho' my child went away.

"Going on a little farther He (Yeshua) fell on his face, praying,
"My Father! If possible, let this cup pass from me! Yet – not what I want,
but what you want."

Matthew 26:39 *(CJB)*

SEEING GREY

white is black and black is white
feeling hopeless but have to fight
looking to the future, but only see the past
my clarity is overcast

i go outside but want to hide
opened, yet remain inside
giving warmth while feeling cold
only young but feeling old

looking up while feeling down
trying to smile when i want to frown
confidence, filled with doubt
silently, i want to shout

acting happy when i'm sad
making sense but going mad
laughing when i 'm not amused
understanding, but oh so confused

accepting yet i can't condone
surrounded yet so alone
dry eyed but yet i cry
single thoughts multiply

tired, but very awake
strong but feel i'm gonna break
feeling wrong but know i'm right
white is black, black is white

My son's own poem written at the start of his healing.

"For the Messiah did not send me to immerse but to proclaim the Good News – and to do it without relying on 'wisdom' that consists of mere rhetoric, so as not to rob the Messiah's execution-stake of its power."
1 Corinthians 1:17 (CJB)

"As for me, God forbid that I should boast about anything except the cross of our Lord Jesus Christ."
Galatians 6:14 (NLT)

"God cancelled the record that contained the charges against us. He took it and destroyed it by nailing it to Christ's cross."
Colossians 2:14

Only One Cross

In this world we will have tribulation,
that's our common lot after all.
We suffer from all the effects of sin
that began with th'Edenic Fall.

Sin, we are told, is the sharp sting of death,
so we suffer from all of its ills
but to cure the actual cause of these
are no policies, med'cines, pills.

One Man alone could stand perfectly there
before God our Father's great throne.
He paid the price that we could never pay,
just His sinless blood could atone.

The Cross that He bore was a selfless one,
Son of God suffered there for me.
So if our trials seem too hard to bear,
that's th'effects of our sin you see.

Christ broke sin's power, and mortality,
rising up from the dark tomb's lair,
He pulled out the sting of grim death for us
no longer to hold us all there.

Our sufferings here are but temporal
and we brought them to Earth's domain
God in His Mercy sent His only Son
Eternity's harvest to gain.

continued…

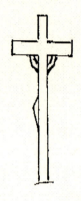

The Cross towers over all History
and calls ALL to come for that blood
spilled by the One who thought not of Himself
but died there for a stubborn brood.

Speak not of your suffering as your 'cross'
we suffer for ourselves alone!
Come follow Christ, take up His Cross today
tell others He died to atone.

"For the house, when under construction, was built of stone prepared at the quarry; so that no hammer, chisel or iron tool of any kind was heard in the house while it was being built."
1Kings 6:7 (CJB)

"But can God actually live with human beings on the earth? Why, heaven itself, even the heaven of heavens, cannot contain you; so how much less this house I have built?"
2 Chronicles6: 18

"Therefore Adonai himself will give you people a sign: the young woman (or virgin) will become pregnant, bear a son and name him 'Immanu El' {God is with us}."
Isaiah 7:14

"Yosef, son of David, do not be afraid to take Miryam home with you as your wife; for what has been conceived in her is from the Ruach Ha Kodesh (Holy Spirit). She will give birth to a son, and you are to name him Yeshua, {which means 'Adonai saves'} because he will save his people from their sins."
Matthew 1:20-21

Living Stones

King Solomon built the Temple
so that God would dwell here with men.
He took every stone from the quarry
to fashion and shape it, and then
place it with care and precision
into its special space.
With noiseless skill each stone would be placed
where no other could take its place.

God also takes 'stones' from the quarry
of this world and our mortal race,
to work with great skill and much patience
His dear Son's image to trace
on these stones that are fashioned and shaped
in the quarry of life's demands,
then placed in that unique space in the Church
by God's power – no human hands.

For the quarry is noisy and dirty,
like the lives of the 'stones' it gives,
but the Temple is built in quiet
where God and Yeshua live.
'Not might, nor power, but my Spirit
will build this Temple of mine.'
The Creator works without ceasing or rest
to fashion His family line.

continued…

"'Sing daughter of Tziyon; rejoice! For, here I am coming; and I will live among you,' says Adonai."
"Be silent, all humanity, before Adonai; for he has been roused from his holy dwelling."
Zechariah 2:14, 17. *(CJB)*

"I saw no temple in the city, for Adonai, God of heaven's armies, is its temple, as is the Lamb."
Revelation 21:22

East, West, Jews, Gentiles and children,
women and men side by side,
being shaped by God's hand in this life.
His Son's Temple will be long and wide.
Are you aware of the chisel
He wields in your life thro' His love?
Did you know that He's made there a space for you,
a space that will 'fit like a glove'?

All the pain and the failure of life
is the dust of the quarry, you see.
But the rocks can become special stones
He's redeemed – yes! even you and me.
There's a space shaped for you in His Temple
'cos He makes you to fit there, just you.
If you let Him be your stone-mason Divine,
He'll work 'til He's honed you right through.

When Solomon built the Temple
to glorify God on the earth,
it prefigured the Church of Immanuel
that began on the Day of His Birth.

"The blood you have smeared on your doorposts will serve as a sign. When I see the blood, I will pass over you. This plague of death will not touch you..."
Exodus 12:13 *(NLT)*

"Look! There is the Lamb of God who takes away the sin of the world."
John 1:29 *(NLT)*

Passover

Sacrificial lamb
sprinkled blood on door lintels
Death passed over homes

Lamb of God's red blood
shed to cover all my sin
Passover to life.

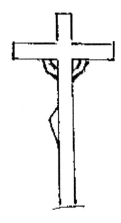

"Don't be quick to get angry for (only) fools nurse anger."
Ecclesiastes 7:9 *(CJB)*

"He who is quick-tempered does stupid things, and one who does vile things is hated."
Proverbs 14:17

Angry With God

When I was three, I fell off my chair.
My mum picked me up and I pulled her hair.

When I was six, I fell off my trike.
My father lifted me, I kicked his bike.

Mother and Father still smiled at me,
they held me close and gently chided me.

Now I'm grown and don't think as a child,
recall how hurts stopped me from being wild,

tamed my strong will, taught me of danger,
made me think of others, kin and stranger.

Life still has dealt some painful rebuts
and I want to kick to relieve my hurts.

With hindsight I see that's unfair and
regret what I did when I fell from my chair.

"Adonai, you are kind and forgiving, full of grace toward all who call on you."
Psalm 86:5 (CJB)

"Forgive us what we have done wrong, as we too have forgiven those who have wronged us."
Matthew 6:12

"For if you do not forgive others their offences, your heavenly Father will not forgive yours."
Matthew 6:1- 15

Can This Be True?

Forgiveness? A sword
to open some painful wounds.
Lets poison run out.

"The Lord is slow to anger and rich in unfailing love, forgiving every kind of sin and rebellion. Even so, He does not leave sin unpunished..."
Numbers 13:18 (NLT)

"When you forgive this man, I forgive him too. And when I forgive him...I do so with Christ's authority..."
2 Corinthians 2:10

I Saw a Man...

The first time I saw Him
He hung on a tree
on Calvary Hill, and I knew
That as it spilled down
It was for me, that blood.

The next time I saw him
He sat in his shop
In Jerusalem's Jewish part.
My heart all but stopped!
He'd survived the Holocaust.

I saw him a third time,
in war-torn Iraq,
interviewed by the BBC.
The dictator's men
bathed his back, with acid.

Each instance I saw Him
His face was the same
Suff'ring and beauty entwined
No anger, self or bitter view
Just, "Father Forgive...
They know not what they do."

"'Did you notice my servant Job, that there's no-one like him on earth…?'"
***Job 1:8** (CJB)*

"Trusting is being confident of what we hope for, convinced about things we do not see." ***Hebrews 11:1***

"Each one of these people of faith died not yet having in hand what was promised, but still believing. How did they do it? They saw it way off in the distance, waved their greeting, and accepted the fact that they were transients in this world… you can see why God is so proud of them and has a City waiting for them."
***Hebrews 11:13-16** (The Message)*

Job's Triumph

Consider God's servant, Job,
a man who'd got it together!
He never met Christ in the flesh
yet said, "I know my Redeemer…"

"Man born of woman will die –
he comes forth like a flow'r then fades…"
Since Job had such grasp of wisdom
God knew that with sin he'd not trade.

Job's wife said: "Curse God and die…"
Her husband just smiled and replied:
"Think of the good received from God,
Let's be patient now," and he sighed,

for Job's friends could not understand
why he "through the waters" must go.
They all needed explanations
whilst Job knew, with God it's not so.

"Faith is the substance of things not seen…"
the Apostle would say in his day.
If we need examples to help us see
what this means, surely Job shows the way.

"On the third day, Esther put on her royal robes and stood in the inner courtyard of the king's palace... 'What is it you want?' the king asked her."
Esther 5:1, 3 (CJB)

"Towards evening there came a wealthy man from Ramatayin [Arimathea] named Yosef, who was himself a disciple of Yeshua. He approached Pilate and asked for Yeshua's body, and Pilate ordered it to be given to him..."
Matthew 27:57-58

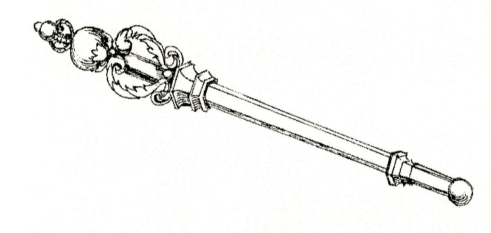

For Such a Time…

Queen Esther needed courage
to go and ask the King
if he'd attend her banquets.
She'd make Hanani sing there
about his evil plans
to wipe God's people out.
She knew the King could kill her,
just raise his hands or shout, but
she had come for such a time as this.

Joseph of Arimathea
gave the tomb where Christ was laid.
We hear no more of Joseph,
does more need to be said?
He had come for such a time as this.

Some may look for greatness
and fame in the eyes of men
Some receive great honour
for their deeds.

Others remain faithful
in a day when smaller things
go unnoticed in the ferment of the age.
"Who knows but that you
are come for such a time as this."

"The Kingdom of Heaven is like a mustard seed… It is the smallest of all the seeds, but when it grows up it is larger than any garden plant and becomes a tree, so that the birds flying about come and nest in its branches."
Matthew 13:32 (CJB)

"I tell you, if you have trust as tiny as a mustard seed, you will be able to say to this mountain, 'Move from here to there!' and it will move: indeed nothing will be impossible for you."
Matthew 17:20-21

A Diamonte is a poem in the shape of a diamond.
It moves from the subject at the top to a different, maybe opposite subject at the bottom.
The route:
Line 1: Noun (subject 1)
Line 2: Two adjectives describing subject 1
Line 3: Three participles ending in 'ing,' telling about subject 1
Line 4: Four nouns – 2 relate to subject 1 and 2 relate to subject 2
Line 5: Three participles, ending in 'ing,' about subject 2
Line 6: Two adjectives describing subject 2
Line 7: Noun (subject 2)

The Mustard Seed

Faith
small vulnerable
believing trusting wavering
object God substance objective
hoping fearing reaching
materialised seen
Proof

"I call on heaven and earth to witness against you today that I have presented you with life and death, the blessing and the curse. Therefore, choose life so that you will live, you and your descendants, loving Adonai your God, paying attention to what He says and clinging to Him – for that is the purpose of your life."
Deuteronomy 30:19-20 (CJB)

"Where is the way to the dwelling of light?"
Job 38:19 (NKJV)

"Go through the narrow gate; for the gate that leads to destruction is wide and the road broad and many travel it; but it is a narrow gate and a hard road that leads to life, and only a few find it."
Matthew 7:13-14 (CJB)

The Known Way

God said: "Let there be light"
and there was.
He made the whole Creation
by His laws.
Yeshua says: "I am the Light,
I am the Way.
Follow Me before the night
replaces day."
Be transformed by renewal
of your mind.
We follow vile ways
when we are blind.
The world is dark, the Way
is hard to find
but the Creator is
wonderfully kind.
Destruction's way is wide
and many run
along that way of death
that looks like fun.
But beauty turns to ashes
on that way
and joy has turned to mourning
by break of day.
I walked that way before
and longed to flee.
And then I heard Him say
"Come! Follow Me."
I did! and never have
looked back.
The Way of Life I love
and nothing lack.

Come On!

"As Yeshua walked by the Lake Kinneret [Sea of Galilee], he saw two brothers who were fishermen, Shim'on Kefa [Peter] and his brother Andrew... Yeshua said to them, 'Come after me and I will make you fishers for men.' At once they left their nets and went with him. Going on from there, he saw two other brothers, Ya'akov [James] and Yochanan [John], sons of Zavdai [Zebedee]... and he called them. At once they left the boat and their father and went with Yeshua."
Matthew 4:18-22 (CJB)

"Later Yeshua went out and saw a tax-collector named Levi [Matthew] sitting in his tax-collection booth; and he said to him 'Follow me!' He got up, left everything and followed him."
Luke 5:27-28

"They were at supper, and the adversary had already put the desire to betray him into the heart of Y'hudah [Judas] from K'riot.... As soon as Y'hudah took the piece of matzah, the adversary went into him. 'What you are doing do it quickly!' Yeshua said to him."
John 13:2, 27

*"She went and told those who had been with him, as they were crying and mourning. But when they heard that he was alive and that she had seen him, they wouldn't believe it."***Mark 16:10-11**

Surprised by Truth

Simon was a simple chap,
fisherman by Galilee.
He must have been astonished
when Yeshua said,
"Come and follow Me."
Matthew had a rotten job
at the Inland Revenue.
He received a big surprise
when Yeshua said:
Come, Matthew I want you."

James and John two brothers were,
the strong sons of Zebedee,
mending nets and catching fish
when Yeshua said
"Shalom! Now come with Me."

As twelve men altogether
were called to follow Him.
only one regretted it
when Yeshua said,
"Judas, the light grows dim..."

Eleven men were afraid
when they saw their Master dead.
Depressed and sad they waited
for Yeshua who'd said:

continued...

"The Son of Man will rise now
on the third day, you will see."
Yet again they were astonished
when joyful Mary said
"Most truly it is HE!"

Truly He is ris'n again,
the Redeemer who calls your name.
Let's not feel depressed or sad
because Yeshua said:
"Forever, I'm the same."

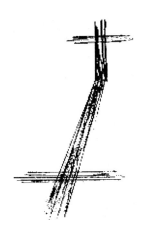

"As for me, I am for peace; but when I speak they are for war!"
Psalm 120:7 (NLT)

"God is our refuge… so we will not fear, even if earthquakes come and the mountains crumble into the sea. Let the oceans roar and foam. Let the mountains tremble as the waters surge."
Psalm 46:1- 3

Escalation

There was a time we're told, when battles were fought
man to man, eye to eye and honour was sought.
But someone invented the gun in his times
and ere long, battles were being fought in lines.

Nature never got the message about war
so it rained just the same making mud and glaur,*
while men trudged thro' mire in far foreign fields
where they fell in their gore, no old-style shields.

Then aeroplanes meant that bombs could be dropped!
with no need to see homes destroyed or life cropped.
No more battles fought eye to eye, man to man
for more can be killed from a distance than
could ever have been killed before
WMDs became battle lore.

The more the earth's population is pruned
the more it explodes and new babies are doomed
to live out short lives in poverty and fears
while man's nature hardens, untouched by tears
or sorrow and grief in this world that's "getting better"?
as we replace one ill with an even worse fetter.

Will we ever admit that we've lost our way,
come humbly to the God of Peace
and learn how to pray?

* glaur is a Scots word for thick mud

"If my sadness could be weighed and my troubles be put on the scales, they would be heavier than all the sands of the sea. That is why I spoke so rashly. For the Almighty has struck me down with his arrows. He has sent his poisoned arrows deep within my spirit. All God's terrors are arrayed against me."

Job 6:2-4 (NLT)

"Where were you when I laid the foundations of the earth?...Can you hold back the movements of the stars?...Can you shout to the clouds and make it rain?..."

Job 38:4, 31, 34

"Then Job replied to the Lord: 'I am nothing - how could I ever find the answers?...'"

Job 40:1

"I am storing up these things, sealing them away within my treasury. I will take vengeance; I will repay those who deserve it. In due time their feet will slip, their day of disaster will arrive and their destiny will overtake them."

Deuteronomy 32:14, 15

Ground Zero

I remember what I was doing that day,
mundane thing – ironing.
"Breaking News…" it said.
Breaking buildings, breaking planes,
breaking bodies, breaking lives,
breaking hearts, breaking dreams
and hopes…
Yes, I remember what I was doing that day,
mundane thing, ironing…

"And wars will break out near and far, but don't panic..."
Matthew 24:6 *(NLT)*

"Anyone who believes in Him will not be disappointed. Jew and Gentile are the same in this respect. They all have the same Lord..."
Romans 10:11-12

"There is no longer Jew or Gentile, slave or free, male or female. You are... one in Christ Jesus."
Galatians 3:28

"Pray this way for kings and all others who are in authority so that we can live in peace and quietness, in godliness and dignity."
1 Timothy 2:2

Elusive Peace

The colour of skin may be black, white, brown
or pink or yellow, even tanned!
but blood in the veins is red as can be
wherever on earth we may stand

The nations are always in uproar now,
the people still suffer en masse
one way or another the price is high
to bring peace to every land

In our countries and towns and our cities
there's much trouble at human hands
vengeance and anger and hatred and spite
keep bias and prejudice fanned

We blame it all on our leaders, of course,
we thought they were gods but they're not
like us they feel and they hurt and they bleed
and fail to enact what they'd planned

Why are the nations in uproar again
the people still grumbling in vain?
could it be that God's rules in His universe
are ignored and our efforts damned?

Cells may be man-made, like prisons, or self made.

"Look! Here I stand at the door and knock. If you hear me and open the door, I will come in, and we will share a meal as friends."
Revelation 3:20 *(NLT)*

"Come to me all you who are struggling and burdened and I will give you rest. Take my yoke upon you and learn from me because I am gentle and humble in heart and you will find rest for your souls. For my yoke is easy and my burden is light."
Matthew 11:28-30 *(CJB)*

Cells

In your cell,
looking at bars or walls,
what do you think of?
Do you think
of those whose lives you hurt?
And of those you loved
who hurt you too?

Is there still
that life within to feel?
Have you confessed
the deeps within?
That which you buried?
Would you? Can you?
Will you?

Only then can
healing begin
for you and for them.

"I did not come to call righteous people, but sinners..." Christ (the Son)
Matthew 9:13 (NLT)

"I have loved you with an everlasting love and with great loving-kindness have I drawn you." Adonai (the Father)
Jeremiah 31:3 (NKJV)

"My child, give Me your heart." Adonai (the Father)
Proverbs 23:26 (CJB)

Remember This

When you fly into a rage
and just can't 'act your age'
Remember this!
God loves you.

When that foul language pours
and you feel you're 'on all fours'
Remember this!
God loves you.

When your mind is 'in the gutter'
"I can't help myself," you mutter
Remember this!
God loves you.

When your life's out of control,
you despise yourself and mourn
Remember this!
God loves you.

When you feel life's just not worth it
Can't make it work or feel you've blown it
Remember this!
God loves YOU
and
Christ died for you.

"Child, give me your heart
and let Me transform you by
My Spirit who will renew
your mind."
Proverbs 23:26 and Romans 12:2 *(my paraphrase)*

Transformation

"I've set two ways before you,
t'wards death or into life.
Choose LIFE and let me lead you
thro' this sad world of strife.

"No-one is beyond My reach.
None too far gone or foul.
It cost My Son His life blood
to make your cleansing real.

"So, ev'ry sin against Me
I've cast to deepest sea.
I'll remember them no more
when you cry out to Me.

"I will show you through my love
what I made you to be,
lift you to a view of life
you could not dream to see.

"This is not magic, dear one,
no wand to make wrong right.
'twill take your life, long or short
to give to you My sight.

"No need to sort your life out
before you come to Me.
Come to Me just as you are,
in time wholeness shall be.

continued…

"I love you, Child. I know you.
You're graven in my wounds.
Receive my Son's fullest LIFE
that's filled with love, no bounds.

"We'll travel thro' this dark place,
thro' ev'ry kind of weather.
You need never fear again,
'I AM' and you together."

"Miryam of Magdala and the other Miryam went to see the grave… the angel said to the women, 'Don't be afraid. I know you are looking for Yeshua, who was executed on the stake. He is not here, because He has been raised, just as He said.'"
***Matthew 28:1, 5, 6** (CJB)*

The poem opposite 'just happened.' The exhibition was in Cambridge and the charcoal sketches were, unknown to me until I saw them, the work of my friend's husband.

The Charcoal Sketch

The town hall buzzed with life as
its majestic room, festooned with
scenes the artists had created for
exhibit, throbbed with murmurs of
admiration, criticism, scepticism,
and cheque books at the ready.

Some paintings would win prizes,
all would surely have admirers
as experts, amateur art lovers
and casual viewers merged,
eavesdropping on comments made,
enjoying myriad displayed scapes.

Two charcoal sketches drew my gaze
telegraphing me from framed
obsequial views where tombstones
rising at varied angles stood,
stark in black and grey, cameoed
'gainst the shaded background of life.
'Twas this backdrop sent the message
from skilfully sketched in houses that,
half circling the cemetery, seemed
higgledy-piggledy yet somehow deemed
agreeably in tune with these memorials
to erstwhile fellow travellers of the town.

'Death amidst life.' Their meaning
spoke clearly for both were quickly
adorned with "SOLD" and the coveted
card of '1st' attached to one while,
at the end of the day, the artists came to
reclaim their finished work and start a new.

"Thus says the High and Exalted One who lives forever, whose name is Holy: 'I live in the high and holy place but also with the broken and humble, in order to revive the spirit of the humble and revive the hearts of the broken ones.'"
Isaiah 53:15 (CJB)

"The eternal God is your refuge and his everlasting arms are under you."
Deuteronomy 33:27 (NLT)

Time Within Eternity

Not apart, but part of.
Sorrow and sadness mixed with joy.
Sickness and infirmity, ruined childhoods,
damaged babies, the ugliness of brutality,
even the beauty that fades,
all this will pass.
We need not 'go' anywhere,
Eternity encapsulates.
Lift up your head and rejoice!
Your passing moments fulfil.
God, who created all things
saw that they were good.
We marred, but He
redeemed them and set a frame
that we call Time.
It lies within Eternity where
He dwells.

"No-one patches an old coat with a piece of unshrunk cloth, because the patch tears away from the coat and leaves a worse hole..."
Matthew 9:16 (CJB)

"...so far as your way of life is concerned, you must strip off your old nature, because your old nature is thoroughly rotted by its deceptive desires, and you must let your spirits and minds keep being renewed, and clothe yourselves with the new nature [of Yeshua the Messiah]..."
Ephesians 4:22-23

New for Old

If you try to patch an old shirt
with a piece of brand new cloth,
The hole made would be bigger soon
and you'd have wasted both.

Religion says; "Appease your god,
make him glad, obey his rule.
That way you'll all earn brownie points
tho' burdened like the mule."

The Jews have their religious rules
and Gentiles all have theirs
but the Gospel shows a different Way
and to mix them just won't wear!!

It's not another religion this,
it's about God's family.
Relationship with Him redeemed
and dwelling in unity.

Yeshua said, "God loves you,
so I've come to set you free.
The Father accepted My sacrifice.
Choose life and come to Me."

We do not earn, win or deserve this
free gift of purest gold.
So, throw old garments on the fire
receive Christ's, new for old.

"You are to love Adonai your God, serve him. cling to him and swear by His Name. He is your praise, and he is your God, who has done for you these great and awesome things, which you have seen with your own eyes."

Deuteronomy 10:20-21 *(CJB)*

Life in the Kingdom

It seems that 'isms' tell me
"You must do this and that…"
Must work for my salvation
to ensure my place - with what?
But there's another Way I'm told
that allows my life to be
free of all such burdens
that would sap my energy.
The 'isms' make me fear for
they force me to be hard
and not let mind or feeling
play the smallest part.
The other Way tells me
that Yeshua did it all
He pioneered the Way
and released me from the pall
of death, to give me now
this life that comes direct
from the Mighty God of Heaven,
making me His own 'elect'.
Eternal life, beginning here *in* me.
So, I don't want 'isms' or philosophy.
Don't want death-dealing gods
fuelled by man's anger
yet cannot lift a finger
if they're made of air or stone
Give me Yeshua any day!
A risen, living Saviour.
So do come and follow on!
Victorious Life's been won
for everyone.

"Pilate asked 'What is truth?'"
John 18:38 *(CJB)*

"He who tells the truth furthers justice, but a false witness furthers deceit."
Proverbs 12:17

*"Don't be troubled. You trust God, now trust in me. There are many rooms in my Father's home, and I am going to prepare a place for you. **If this were not so, I would have told you.**"*
John 14:1-2 *(NLT)*

Truth or Fiction

Her acting never fails to entrance
whether heroine, villain or wench.
She plays ev'ry role with conviction
and audiences love Judi Dench.

His painting is full of such detail,
country scenes and the tools used to tame,
and few folks would fail to respond
to how Constable stroked The Haywain.

In comedy, we don't like to see
ourselves laughed at or in comment rude.
Somehow she always avoids that,
British wit Victoria Wood.

In writing, his plots weave a story
that is not too far fetched to believe.
John Grisham has perfected this art
dark, cold winter nights to relieve.

What is it that makes us respond so
to those things we enjoy most? Forsooth!
It's the same as in God's Word prevails,
we all call it 'the ring of truth'.

"When the woman saw that the tree was good for food, that it had a pleasing appearance and that the tree was desirable for making one wise, she took some of its fruit and ate. She also gave some of it to her husband and he ate. Then the eyes of both of them were opened and they realised that they were naked. So, they sewed fig leaves together to make themselves loincloths. They heard the voice of Adonai, God, walking in the garden at the time of the evening breeze, so the man and his wife hid themselves from the presence of Adonai, God, among the trees in the garden."

Genesis 3:6-8 *(CJB)*

The Un-Masked Ball

When you get your invitation
to this particular ball,
the first thing that you have to do
is admit that God knows it all.

So, there's really no point hiding
or cov'ring all He can see.
God wants to take away all that,
cast it into the deepest sea.

Then you'll meet so many people!
Join in the great Freedom dance,
where all the cover-up is gone,
beauty make-up cannot enhance.

It's the beauty of Yeshua
attributed here to you.
Truth, peace, joy, love and faithfulness,
now our Heavenly revenue!

You won't need any ticket tho'
to attend this splendid ball.
Just tell the angel at the door,
"Yeshua has paid for it all!"

PS. Everyone's invited.

"When it is evening, you say; 'Fair weather ahead,' because the sky is red; and in the morning you say; 'Storm today!' because the sky is red and overcast. You know how to read the appearance of the sky, but you can't read the signs of the times!"

Matthew 16:2-3 *(CJB)*

"For there will be trouble then, worse than there has ever been from the beginning of the world until now, and there will be nothing like it again.... Now let the fig tree teach you a lesson: when its branches begin to sprout and leaves appear, you know that summer is approaching. In the same way, when you see all these things, you are to know that the time is near..."

Matthew 24:21, 32-33

Chaos

An airport goes on Red Alert
"No planes will fly tonight!
It's not our fault," the staff all cry,
"It's weather that stopped your flight.
We know that you're 'in transit'
and need to go on from here
but you just have to accept and know
that you can't, so that's that we fear."

Evil brought down the Twin Towers
the world looked on aghast
"How could this happen in our time?
Let's get back to 'normal' fast."
Tsunami hits eastern lands
people are swamped and lost.
Governments act to send them help
but they cannot stem the great cost.

A hurricane strikes the Crescent
by hours grim misery flows.
People and statesmen are helpless
as the toll of Katrina grows.
Hiroshima, Nagasaki
and world wars one and two
plus all the killing of History,
Do we still think our world is 'new'?

continued…

World systems are all breaking down,
there are plagues, floods, winds and fires.
all these ordeals to avenge the earth
Will we listen as Creation tires?

For the whole of the earth is groaning
at Man's selfishness and greed.
Will we stop grabbing at all we see
and recognise our true need?

God tells us the end will come
and those days will awful be.
We need to see the signs of the times
while He still says "Come unto Me."

For that Day will be terrible
the living will envy the dead.
Take heed, my friend, attend to this
'ere the judgement comes on your head.

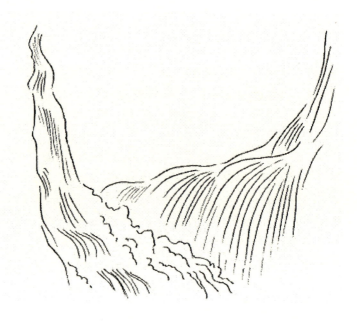

"For the Lord at the centre of the throne will shepherd them, will lead them to springs of living water, and God will wipe every tear from their eyes."
Revelation 7:17 (CJB)

"...His feet like burnished brass refined in a furnace, and His voice like the sound of rushing waters."
Revelation 1:15

The Sound of Many Waters

There's a sound above all others that I love,
and it comes through the many moods of water.

Often it's a gurgling, chuckling sound.
Happy, free water.

It may be turbulent, roaring, warning sound.
Angry water.

Lapping on the shore, with birds-all-bobbing sound.
Peaceful water.

Thundering over rapids or cataract or weir.
Getting-down-to-business water.

Calm, barely rippling sound of fluid movement.
Deep water.

Sound of shower and bath water soothing and refreshing.
Cleansing water.

Taps and wells and sounds of animals lapping.
Living water.

The sounds I love reflect our lives but
there's something even better …

for God is near in all these sounds
"…and the sound of many waters is His voice."

"Aaron shall lay both his hands on the head of the live goat confessing all the iniquities of the children of Israel… putting them on the head of the goat and shall send it away into the wilderness by the hand of a suitable man."
Leviticus 16:21 (CJB)

"'Come now and let us reason together' says the Lord. 'Though your sins be like scarlet, they shall be as white as snow: though they be red like crimson, they shall be as wool.'"
Isaiah 1:18 (NKJV)

"…and among the menorahs, was someone like a Son of Man, wearing a robe down to His feet and a gold band around His chest. His head and hair were as white as snow-white wool…"
Revelation 1:13 (CJB)

A Suitable Man

When they plaited that awful crown of thorns,
and pressed it down hard on your head,
they could not know just how well they fulfilled
all that the Old Covenant said.

You were there in my place, silent and still
like the mute goat at Aaron's hand,
when you bore away all our darkened deeds
to an empty, wilderness land.

On the stake that awaited, nails and spear,
wrath of the Father 'gainst sin,
You were the just sacrifice, pure and clean,
dying there for me midst that din.

The silence, the darkness came at the end.
You died there, and Heaven was still.
The great price had been paid for our ransom,
You'd fulfilled all the Father's will.

And now there at the Father's right hand, Lord
we see you with head white as snow
and white like wool as the prophet had said
when he spoke your Word here below.

It is finished

"Yes! Amen!"

"I am the 'A' and the 'Z' says Adonai,
God of heaven's armies,
the One who is, who was and who is coming."
***Revelation 1:8** (CJB)*

New Creation

People could fight, but they don't,
could war with each other and kill,
but the love of God spread abroad
in their hearts, elicits such love for His Will,
that they live side-by-side in their lands,
till the ground, manufacture their wares,
so that all people everywhere eat of the fat
as they laugh and rejoice to God's praise.
Skin colours all mix in a folk-scape,
the shades of Creation all round.
Children and animals romp and play
while rivulets water the ground.
Light never dims and there's no sun to burn.
When rain falls we lift up our face
rejoicing, refreshing, dancing and singing
of God, who's done all by His grace.
A hush falls as angels appear!
Someone's approaching we see.
It's Yeshua coming to stay with us
The One who made all this for me
and you, when He paid the great price
of our ransom, deliverance from all evil's pains.
No more hurts, no more tears, no more death,
that all finished when He broke those chains.
"Will everyone be there?" we ask.
That's each individual's choice
The Scriptures of God say, "Come unto Me..."
Each one must respond to His voice.
We enter a glorious reception,
wearing a brand new robe.
His righteousness only clothing each one
of His people, the children of God.

Come On!

"Then I saw a new Heaven and a new earth, for the old heaven and the old earth had disappeared...and I saw the Holy City, the new Jerusalem, coming down from God out of Heaven like a beautiful bride prepared for her husband... 'Look! the home of God is now among His people! He will live with them and they will be His people. God himself will be with them. He will remove all their sorrows and there will be no more death or sorrow or crying or pain. For the old world and its evils are gone forever.'"
Revelation 21:1-4 *(NLT)*

Alphabetical Index of Poems

Printed in the United Kingdom
by Lightning Source UK Ltd.
108035UKS00001B/196-213